MILES ON THE SOUL

Farhat Ehsan

BookLeaf Publishing

Presentation by *BookLeaf Publishing*

Web: www.bookleafpub.com

E-mail: info@bookleafpub.com

ISBN: 9789395969567

First edition 2022

DEDICATION

Mama, my grandmother - the woman who thought me unconditional love.

PREFACE

I think, therefore I am.

WHO AM I

Sometimes I wonder, who, who am I?
Do I speak the truth or do I lie?

Do I relinquish or do I rebel?
Do I stay quiet or do I yell?

Am I a saint or a sinner?
An underdog or a winner?

Am I a cause or an effect?
Should I ponder, or deflect?

If I am a mystery, who can solve me?
Should I even try, or just let it be?

Do I stay hidden or do I reveal?
Do I go with what I think or how I feel?

Am I a sum of all the paths that I have taken?
Thoughts that I let in or the ones I have shaken?

Do these questions also keep you awake at night?
Do you also live in shades of grey, instead of black
and white?

The thin line between right and wrong..
Is it linear enough to tell the weak and strong?

Guess we'll never know all the answers
Life's a pounding drum and we are nothing but
dancers

So gather around the fire and keep shuffling your feet
You gotta put up with life's ever-changing beat

And maybe over the years you'll get the hang of it
And the answers will unfold bit by bit

Because if we had to live by a wise man's words;
Life can only be lived forwards and understood..
backwards.

DIVERGING PATHS

Middle of July, under the night sky
In the back of your pick up truck, you lie

Tailing fresh rain, gazing the stars
Has it been minutes or hours?

So tell me what do you see
Is it a map of all that could be?

The diverging paths and the people left behind
Suddenly all the street signs of your childhood you find

All the destinations that you didn't reach
All the lessons life couldn't teach

All the versions of yourself that couldn't be
All the possibilities that you now see

All the journeys that you couldn't take
All the choices that you couldn't make

Where would you be if you had taken that road instead?
What if the silence was replaced by all the right things
said?

Do you see all your future selves staring at you?
Questioning you for all you did and didn't do..

It's all too much, you shut your eyes
Reminders of all those unspoken goodbyes

Breathe, calm down, listen to me.... Hey!
It's important to know what I'm going to say..

They say you always find your way
Even in chaos, it will be as clear as day

And now you're right where you ought to be
That's the funny thing about destiny

THE ANSWER

Oh my silly heart!
Let me take you back to the start

When you were young and free
Did they say what would make you happy?

Would it be power, money or fame?
Isn't the pursuit always the same?

Would it be people validating your choices?
Or getting acclaimed by a dozen voices?

Would it be approval of those around you?
Pat on the back for every little thing you do

Would it be driving a fancy car?
Would it be becoming a super star?

What would it be, tell me my friend
Have your struggles come to an end?

Today, when you have it all
Shining accolades mounted on your wall

Tell me how do you really feel?
Did you get the promised deal?

You bow your head, lost deep in thought
You wish it was enough, but it is not

You are still looking for peace you say
Perhaps there's still some other way

Those razor-sharp eyes now appear glazed
But the universe isn't surprised, it stays unfazed

It has witnessed countless humans before
Who had everything they desired.. and more

And yet they couldn't find the bliss
Because what they didn't know, was this;

You're searching for answers all around
And yet muting your internal sound

Counting on others to make you feel
Not just happy but to make you heal

Alas! This is where it all went wrong
The power rested within you all along

DOMESTICATED ANIMAL

I'm looking at a world that's full of shades
It's hard to tell clubs from spades

Show me a life that's soaked in color
Leave out the parts that make it duller

Take me to the place where people find answers
To myths of demons and fire dancers

If man had to trade away his sanity
In order to bring back dying humanity

A fool would be better than a thousand scholars
Give me devotion instead of starched collars

If society decided to show it's scars
In the quietly lit sundown hours

We'd watch the ashes of faith burn
Our souls perish to point of no return

I had a dream, this is how it goes
It was a place that no one knows

In that town, everyone was a stranger
I ran to shelter as I sensed the danger

I built a cave, retrieved inside
I was a mystery to their ailing pride

I locked myself in and became king of the world
No one could see my flaws, my imperfections hurled

My silence was strong, it kept them intrigued
My fears were guarded, a cautious breed

Then something strange happened and changed it all
It's like I had crossed a mirror wall

I opened my heart and let the feelings in
And that's the bravest I have ever been

There was a voice and this is all it asked
What holds you back, what keeps you masked?

Why don't you light your passion ablaze?
What are you doing with your numbered days?

I decided to let go and give in to fate
Yes, my revelation was a heavy bait

I could hear a beat in my heart of stone
It gave me a high I had never known

I forgot the differences and began to give
The shackles fell, every fiber in me started to live

I was an animal, born-free
But the world had finally tamed me

That was my purpose, I finally found
To be domesticated instead of being a hound

To open my heart, to free my brain
To learn to give a purpose to pain

Now I walk the ocean, on earth I run
They call me a perfectionist but I'm not the only one

Alas! I had been a total fool
To think humanity is anything but a lover's rule

THE PRICE

Between right and wrong when your morals are caught
Reasoning doesn't seem worth a shot
Where reality is just a thought
Fiction is more real than not

When plans disappear without a trail
The storm makes it hard to sail
Your faith is numb, your hands are pale
Every truth is behind a veil

When the tip of ice berg starts to melt
You doubt everything you've ever felt
Tired of playing the hand you're dealt
Returning despondent every time you've knelt

When voices bawl inside your head
Choking on all the words you've ever said
In an altar where monsters are locked and fed
Pain doesn't stop even if you try playing dead

Sinking deep, barely coming up for air
Losing all sense of time in despair
Comatosed, yet somehow painfully aware
Your nemesis mocks you in a stare

In the middle of sleep and staying awake
Putting all your promises at stake
Sometimes it's more than you can take
Wondering how long before you break

Stranded miles away from sanity
Where delusion is the only reality
You pay a price too high for vanity
To save humans from humanity

THE ROAD AHEAD

Where does this road go
Hit the paddle, who wants to know

Staring at a world full of opportunities
Buckle up, turn in the key

You've got a fancy car
Top up the tank, gotta drive it far

Pull over, get in the fast lane
Got nothing to lose, nothing to gain

Crack down the window, feel the wind
Of places over the globe that you've pinned

Watch the passing lights in rear view
If someone asks where you headed to

Take out the map and point to anywhere
Tell them you're going there

Keep driving, lose track of hours
Below the night sky full of stars

Toss the coin, take a turn
Forget all the rules they made you learn

Get lost in paths that once you knew
Let the world surprise you

They say it's thrill of the chase
Stay directionless, drive in haze

You've got an empty road ahead
The journey has begun, all farewells said

Leaving all the worries behind
Only thoughts of tomorrow on your mind

Who knows when will you stop
Till the world ends or till you drop

A SIGN

Times are hard, she's a little lost
Her dreams are bleary in the frost

All she wants is a sign
To know that she'll be fine

In the world that's cold and huge
She'd be able to find a refuge

Perhaps stumble across a shelter
Find a smile that will melt her

Growing up is hard she knows
She drops her head, looks down at her toes

She's scared and weak but in her nightmares
She finds a voice, a shadow that cares

The moment stops, she follows the lead
With beating heart, she begins to read

The message that the stranger holds
A gentle hand that unfolds

She's survived, she's done it before
Again this time, maybe once more

She thinks of a better tomorrow
Where world wouldn't know of sorrow

Where tomorrows are better than yesterdays
Where no one's heard of clouded greys

The dreams that seem distant for now
Deep down she believes somehow

For all those who fall down and stand
There exists a promised land

HANDS OF TIME

Everyone has a surreptitious side
Closet of skeletons they want to hide

Places that they don't want to go
Scars that they can't afford to show

Memories that would blur never
A moment that lasted forever

A fleeting thought you try to outrun
And suddenly the past comes undone

Sunless skies or cloudy hearts
Flashbacks gleaming in a million parts

A gentle smile, a hint of a face
Taking you back to a happy place

It's a cable car on track so fast
Yesterdays turning to a fuzzy past

This minute and hour, this too shall pass
For they say life is an hour-glass

It's funny you think one would learn
Walk away, not to look back or turn

Since it’s goodbyes that we hate the most
Yet paint sunsets, ships sailing away from coast

Maybe one day we’ll meet again
Foggy morning in pouring rain

Over coffee, chat for a few
Speak of life and how we do

Remember the years that we lost
Settling again in heavy frost

And once again we’ll build an empire of photographs
to stay
Till mist of time decides to wash it away

IN HER WORLD

n a distant place, he wears a vacant face
With a happy trace, her heart begins to race

He's trying hard to cope
She's an innocent victim of hope

His soul is heavy, burdened with sorrow
Her heart is young, yearning for tomorrow

His repeated nightmares, muffled screams
She has big plans, beautiful dreams

He's running out of bait, as his boat sinks
A calm shore awaits, that's what she thinks

His night is long, waiting for sun to rise
Her delusion is strong, crazy shine in her eyes

Life brings him down, before he finishes to grieve
Reality is a happy town, she's eager to believe

He's afraid to open the door, terrified to let the storms in
She's restless to step in downpour, welcome the feeling on her skin

Crippled faith makes him weak in the knees

She wears her heart on her sleeves

He's tasted all flavors of regret
She's ready to forgive and forget

When the planet brings them one to one
Who will hold the loaded gun

They're both a progeny of their circumstances
The universe is thrilled as the devil dances

But reality my friend, is quite different
She'd change your world if you met her

Give you strength to put up a fight
Make you pull through the darkest night

Speak of hope with fire in her tone
Introduce you to passion that you've never known

Her spirit is wild, it will intoxicate you
Make you believe that all your dreams can come true

With her if only you walk for a mile
She will bring you your brightest smile

Take a breath, now read it slow
What comes next is important to know

To the world very little she shows
Deep inside only one thing she knows

What's another troubled heart in a crowd of madness
The world doesn't need to see her sadness

With dazzling words, she shows her strength
Angelic hand to push you to any length

Her life is vibrant, think you might
She's easy to read, a happy person right?

But for you here's a little surprise
At first it took her a several tries

Now behind recklessly beautiful smile she can easily hide
She killed her feelings, she's dead inside

METAMORPHOSIS

Tick tock, around the clock
You are just a bird in the flock

Every day you set on the same march
Under all the weight, your back begins to arch

One day you wake up and the noise is too much
Your head and reality are totally out of touch

You pack your bags and decide to do
Something surprising, totally out of the blue

You set on a journey to find yourself
Like discovering a book on the bottom shelf

But to find yourself, first you have to get lost
As sun rises in the wake of morning frost

You leave the roads and take the trails
Till city skyline behind you pales

You cross the streams, to songs of birds
You start hearing the nature instead of words

The waterfalls rinse the civilization off of you
The weight has lifted, you're something new

The sun sets behind the snow-laden peak

It begins to unravel the answers you seek

You gaze at the stars, you feel the earth
A universe so majestic, it feels like rebirth

In front of the mighty mountains you stand
You realize you've been building castles in sand

What you thought will stay forever and on
In a blink of eye, it will all be gone

What are your worries, what are your dreams
The regrets, the hopes, the elaborate schemes

Many a men have walked this land before
All of them washed like footsteps on the shore

You're just a speck in galaxy so huge
This is your reality, your only refuge

The wisdom in wilderness should set you free
Stop building empires and let yourself be

In this moment alone, all the secrets lie
You lose your cocoon and morph into a butterfly

UNLEARN

It's time to revise some general rules
Equip yourself with new survival tools

Unlearn few things that you've been told
Let go of the weight you're trying to hold

Don't settle for less, you're worth more
Don't knock twice on the same door

Stop trying to fix the damaged ones
Don't tiptoe between the loaded guns

Quit explaining yourself to those who don't
understand
Stop trying to control what's not in your hand

Let go of the fears etched in your head
Break free from the lies that you've been fed

Embrace yourself in your full glory
Don't be afraid to write your story

You are madness, you are magic
Without you, their life would be tragic

Set them ablaze with your desire
Don't let anyone put out your fire

Unlearn that failure is the worst
Learn to leave your comfort zone first

Unlearn to keep watering the dead grass
Learn to wave goodbye, nod and pass

Unlearn to carry baggage through every turn
Learn that it's okay to let some bridges burn

Unlearn to give away your peace of mind
Learn to have your boundaries defined

Unlearn that you need to fit in the crowd
Learn the word esteem, erase the word proud

Unlearn to apologize for your choices
Learn to mute the unnecessary voices

Unlearn that life is a race
Learn to follow your own pace

Unlearn the notion that silence is strong
Learn to tell right from wrong

Unlearn that emotions are for weak to show
Learn to let your expression flow

Learn to let the good ones in
The ones that want to see you win

The rest of them are just people you know
Learn that they will come and go

Unlearn to go out of your way
Learn that the real ones will always stay

Unlearn that you've to please them all
Learn to say no while standing tall

Unlearn to focus on their love and loathe
Learn to invest in your personal growth

Yes, unlearning is one of the hardest parts
But this is where your evolution starts

STRANGERS (ONE)

They write about strangers becoming friends
But that is not how every story ends

Let me tell you a different tale
Where life takes you on an unusual trail

This is the one where they fall apart
Although that's not where we start

She was fire, he was the air
Both would make a dynamic pair

He would fan her flames higher
When together, they were a live wire

Poles apart, like day and night
They would argue, they would fight

But whenever she needed, he was by her side
Through thick and thin, through every ride

Her ambitions were high, her dreams were grand
She wouldn't back down once she'd taken a stand

He took life at a steadier speed
Trusting wherever his fate might lead

If she was the heart, he was the head
She was fuelled by passion, he was reason instead

Like Yin and Yang, they were integral to each
Together they had a lot of potential to reach

One day she decided she had to leave
Step out of comfort zone, bigger things to achieve

The endless possibilities that kept her awake
To chase the life that was hers to make

She told him of the vision she had
Thought he would cheer her on and be glad

But all she got was silence in return
This was the moment she had to discern

At times, you've to pick and choose
Something you keep, something you lose

She packed her bags and set out to explore
Scared to enter the world she hadn't seen before

At the terminal, for him she waited
But the departure came as it was fated

She took the train to follow her dreams
The path was clear in her head it seems

The unsaid goodbye did leave some pain
But just like that, they became strangers again

REUNION (STRANGERS-TWO)

Years passed and she had built an empire
But there was no one to fuel her fire

She would think of him often though
Now he was just someone she used to know

One day as she sat in a coffee shop
Suddenly in front of her, he came to stop

Paralyzed in place, she couldn't believe her eyes
In her head she had rehearsed a thousand goodbyes

He gave a smile as closer he walked
Sat next to her table and for hours they talked

Turns out he had come all these years ago
She waited on the other end, little did he know

But life had to send them their separate ways
For growth to happen, in the next phase`

Today, years later, her kingdom stands
He has all the wisdom in his hands

But now her fire is turning blue
The voice of reason in him is quieter too

She is where she always wanted to be
All possibilities unlocked, she holds the key

He took the path more suited for him
He acted on logic, never on whim

But now he has a sudden desire
To bring back the passion, ignite her fire

For his wisdom is nothing if he doesn’t dare
She used to be fire, but he was her air

Its like they’re back at the station again
All those years ago, whistle of approaching train

Then all becomes quiet, time freezes
But this time the moment he seizes

In her dying flame, suddenly something zings
As she finds the wind beneath her wings

Still yin and yang, still poles apart
But just like that, they go back to start

SILENCE

Is silence strong? Or is it weak?
This is the mystery that I seek

Walking away silently from a fight means you're strong?
But it is weakness if you don't point out something that's wrong

Are the silent ones always so brave?
Or sometimes they're just so scared that they cave?

They say silence can do no harm
Sometimes it's even a part of the charm

But what if there are words you have to say
And there is absolutely no other way

Breaking your silence can in turn defend
A criminal or a culprit, that will depend

Or like a moment you've to let someone know
Keep them forever and let them go

What if it is something you've to voice
To help someone make the right choice

What if it is as grave as someone holding a knife
And you have just the words to save their life

What purpose is it that silence serves?
Yes it can help you calm your nerves

Sometimes when there's chaos in your mind
If you don't seek help, you're being unkind

Sometimes you just have to speak to a friend
To let it out, to get your misery to end

So no, it's not about staying quiet or always chiming
It has a lot to do with your tone and timing

The secret is to master your tongue
For every scholar was once hot headed and young

With time you learn the power of silence and speech
Because true strength lies in a little of each

They say silence is important but so are words
For you're human, not a mockingbird

OBSESSION WITH FOREVER

I wonder why can't people live in here and now
They're either in the past or future somehow

Life is like an hourglass
Every little moment will pass

If you don't cherish the moment you're in
It's like giving up before you begin

You think you are wise, you think you're clever
But what is your obsession with forever?

Life is a collection of moments and nothing more
You only have counted days to hold the floor

If you spend them worrying about yesterday and tomorrow
You are wasting time you're allowed to borrow

You're worried that a moment won't last
And before you know it's in the past

So stop and let your perspective shift
Every moment you get is a gift

Time is an illusion and every illusion shatters
Now is what you get and that's all that matters

Who has seen forever, it could be non-existent
But if you want, you could live eternity in an instant

BE YOUR OWN HERO

If I told you there's a recipe for your peace of mind
Something that people spend years to find

And no, there's no catch, I'll even tell you for free
The rest is on you, to practice it and be

All your hopes and your expectations
Don't put their weight on your relations

Don't be scared to refuse
The things that you could lose

Don't give anybody the power to bring you down
You're the queen, you fix your crown

You are the master of your own fate
Don't get distracted, don't fall for the bait

You're the firework, you're dynamite
Go paint the sky neon bright

You are the anchor, you're the force
Choose happiness, you're your own source

Let go of all the fears that weigh you down
You define the rules, you built this town

Be your own cheerleader, carry your own boombox
Keep collecting the flowers, just ignore the rocks

You are the playwright, you write your own story
Make it sensational, paint yourself in all your glory

Be your own hero, your own white knight
You're the thunder, you're the light

So go on, grace your throne in the golden tower
You, my darling hold all the power

Count on yourself, after all you know it best
Invest in yourself as long as your heart beats in your chest

THE MASQUERADE

In a distant town, she was out to explore
When she came across a curtained door

Someone summoned her in and handed her a mask
What is this place, she wanted to ask

They told her she could be whoever she wanted to be
So she silently followed, as she was curious to see

The lights were dim, there was a neon glow
Everyone followed a rhythm, they danced slow

Each person wore a mask on their face
She thought to herself; what a strange place

Their lips moved, but the voices so hush
They moved swiftly but there was no rush

In the crowd, someone caught her eye
She whispered slowly "where am I?"

He pulled her in for a slow dance
It truly was a state of trance

Her mask was red, his was blue
Who was this person, she had no clue

She slowed down and followed his lead
What was on his mind, she tried to read

He had an enigma, he had a charm
She twirled gracefully around his arm

The moment was magic, there was poise
What a beautiful stranger, said her inner voice

She knew in the moment she felt free
She felt seen and so did he

They could both clearly see
What all it could turn out to be

So she pulled away as she sensed the danger
Like a moth she was drawn to the stranger

Alas! Here comes one of the saddest parts
They were both afraid to open their hearts

Once again the fear of getting hurt won
So they decided it's better to run

Behind their masks they continued to hide
Even though they desired the same thing inside

She turned and ran towards the exit line
When she stumbled across a sign

As she read the name of the place
Her heart suddenly began to race

Frantic, towards the door she hurled
The place was called nothing but “the world”

MILES ON THE SOUL

The innocence, the tranquility, where did it all go?
What growing up does, how could you ever know?

Do you ever sit down and think?
All the simple things gone in a blink

When you would jump in puddles after rain
Scraping your arm would be the only pain

As a child, your world was small
Your mom came rushing every time you had a fall

Now you own a fleet of cars
But your soul is full of scars

When the loss was not of people but a toy
When a simple candy would be your biggest joy

When you would run mile after mile
Yet your face held nothing but a smile

Now you're tired all the time
Missing your multi-vitamin feels like a crime

When home was chasing mom and dad between pillow hills
Not a mortgage and never-ending bills

How many kind faces that you used to adore
They don't walk this earth anymore

And you desperately look for a rewind
If only! Oh, If only.. life was this kind

Memories remain, laced with tears
Fragments of you, lost through the years

I understand now that you can never be whole
And this realization has put miles on my soul

www.ingramcontent.com/pod-product-compliance
Lightning Source LLC
Chambersburg PA
CBHW051742130826
49812CB00033B/963
* 9 7 8 9 3 9 5 9 6 9 5 6 7 *